RECORD BUSTERS
BUGS

CLIVE GIFFORD

WAYLAND

Published in paperback in 2016 by Wayland
Copyright © Wayland 2016

Wayland
An imprint of Hachette Children's Group
Part of Hodder & Stoughton
Carmelite House, 50 Victoria Embankment
London EC4Y 0DZ

Editor: Nicola Edwards
Designer: Basement 68

A catalogue record for this book is available
from the British Library.

ISBN: 978 0 7502 8908 5
Library e-book ISBN: 978 0 7502 8514 8

Printed in China
10 9 8 7 6 5 4 3 2 1

Wayland is a division of
Hachette Children's Group,
an Hachette UK company.
www.hachette.co.uk

Picture credits: Cover: Shutterstock © Dr Morley
Read; p2 Shutterstock © Milena; p4 Shutterstock
© reptiles4all; p5 Shutterstock © Hugh Lansdown;
p6 (l) Shutterstock © edelia, (r) Shutterstock © Dr
Morley Read; p7 Shutterstock © Dr Morley Read; p8
Shutterstock © Suede Chen; p9 (t) Corbis © Stephen
Dalton/Minden Pictures/Corbis, (b) Shutterstock © Dr
Morley Read; p10 Shutterstock © NCG; p11 Shutterstock
© lavoview; p12 Shutterstock © wxin; p13 Shutterstock
© Steve Byland; p14 Shutterstock © Nancy Bauer; p15
Shutterstock © Milena; p16 (l) © Juniors Tierbildarchiv/
Photoshot, (r) Photo: Elizabeth Rogers, (b) Shutterstock
© Tatsiana S; p17 Wikimedia Commons (Daniel Mietchen/
Marek, P; Shear, W; Bond, J); p18 (both) © The Natural
History Museum, London; p19 (l) Shutterstock © Petar
Milevski, (r) © The Natural History Museum, London;
p20 Shutterstock © Eric Isselee; p21 (t) Shutterstock
© Meoita, (b) Shutterstock © John Michael Evan
Potter; p22 Shutterstock © Peteri; p23 Shutterstock
© Sergey Lavrentev; p24 (l) © Eye of Science/Science
Photo Library, (r) Shutterstock © Henrik Larsson; p25
Shutterstock © Henrik Larsson; p26 Shutterstock ©
Dr Morley Read; p27 Shutterstock © Peter Waters; p28
© Alain Beignet / Biosphoto; p29 Shutterstock © Eric
Isselee; p30 Shutterstock © Sergey Lavrentev

Abbreviations used:

m = metres
km = kilometres
cm = centimetres
mm = millimetres
kg = kilogrammes
g = grammes
km/h = kilometres per hour
°C = degrees Centigrade

Tricky words are listed in 'But What
Does That Mean?' on page 31.

WHAT'S INSIDE?

GOLIATH BIRD EATING SPIDER

HEAVIEST SPIDER!

A member of the tarantula family, this spider is a real whopper. Its body can reach almost 20cm and its leg span can measure 28cm – about the size of a dinner plate. They can weigh as much as 170g.

Can you believe it?

Found in swamps and marshes in South America, the Goliath is big enough to eat mice, frogs and birds. Mostly, though, it eats other bugs including large cockroaches.

Male Goliath spiders live for about six years, but females can live for up to 25 years.

CONTENDERS

The giant huntsman spider has a slightly bigger leg span than the Goliath, but only a 5cm-long body. It is less heavy overall.

A huntsman spider snacks on a caterpillar in Australia's Kakadu National Park.

WOW!

THE GOLIATH'S EYESIGHT IS WEAK EVEN THOUGH IT HAS EIGHT EYES. IT SPENDS MUCH OF ITS TIME UNDERGROUND IN ITS BURROW, WHICH IT LINES WITH SILK.

AUSTRALIAN TERMITE

Australian termites work together to build big – really big – nests. How big? Well, some are over 25m in diameter. Others rise up above the ground to heights of 6m.

BIGGEST BUILDER!

Inside this giant termite nest in Australia is a maze of shafts and corridors. These help channel air around the nest to keep it cool.

Can you believe it?

Nests are built by thousands upon thousands of worker termites, all of which are blind. They feel and push around dirt and particles of wood and plants to build their nests.

WOW!

A TERMITE QUEEN CAN LAY 20-30,000 EGGS A DAY AND LIVE FOR UP TO 45 YEARS!

A termite queen can grow to the length of your index finger.

On the other hand...

Some parasitoid wasps get other creatures to build a home for their babies. These wasps inject a spider with chemicals that make the spider spin a sack of silk, called a cocoon, around itself. The wasp lays its eggs in the cocoon. When they hatch, they feed on the poor spider!

FROGHOPPER

If there was an Olympics for bugs, then froghoppers would be high jump champions. They are just 5-7mm long but can jump 100 times higher than their size – up to 70cm.

A brightly-coloured froghopper rests on the stem of a plant.

A froghopper jumps from a leaf. Blink and you'll miss it!

Can you believe it?

Froghoppers catapult themselves upwards using large muscles and two arched parts of their body which act like a spring. These get them moving at a speed of around 4m per second. That's 15 times faster than a jet airliner!

CONTENDERS

Fleas can jump to 20cm high and 33cm forward thanks to their large rear legs. They spring off their toes into the air.

WOW!

FROGHOPPERS COVER THEMSELVES IN BUBBLY FOAM BLOWN OUT OF THE REAR OF THEIR BODIES WHEN THEY ARE YOUNG. THE FOAM PROTECTS THEM FROM PREDATORS.

The foam made by the froghoppers gives them their nickname of 'Spittlebugs'.

9

MONARCH BUTTERFLY

Monarchs are beautiful butterflies that are mostly found in North America. Every August, thousands of them set off on a long-distance journey south into Mexico to find somewhere less cold to live for the winter. Many monarchs fly more than 3,000km.

FURTHEST TRAVELLING!

Can you believe it?

The butterflies hibernate over the winter. When spring comes, they begin their return journey, flying all the way back north again.

Monarch butterflies arriving in Mexico after their long journey south.

Monarchs sip nectar from flowers using their proboscis, a long tube shaped like a drinking straw.

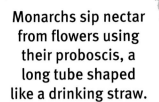

CONTENDERS

Scientists have discovered dragonflies which they think may travel even further, between Asia and Africa every year.

WOW!

LIVING AS AN ADULT BUTTERFLY FOR 6-7 MONTHS MAY NOT SOUND VERY LONG, BUT IT MAKES THE MONARCH ONE OF THE LONGEST-LIVING OF ALL BUTTERFLIES.

CICADA

The cicada family of insects are the noisiest bugs of all. The African cicada generates sounds that have been measured at 107 decibels. That's almost as loud as standing next to a chainsaw!

Can you believe it?

In some parts of the world, such as China, Japan and the US, people cook and eat cicadas.

These cicadas have been stir-fried to make a crunchy nutty-tasting snack.

CONTENDERS

The water boatman is a water insect that is only 2mm long. Despite its small size, it can make a noise that reaches 99 decibels!

WOW!

PERIODICAL CICADAS LIVE UNDERGROUND WHERE THEY FEED ON NUTRIENTS FROM THE ROOTS OF TREES. THEY ONLY COME OUT OF THE GROUND ONCE EVERY 13 OR 17 YEARS.

An African cicada's chirps can be heard over 1.5km away. They create the noise by rubbing little drum-like membranes on their bodies called timbals.

ARCTIC WOOLLY BEAR CATERPILLAR

Caterpillars turn into moths or butterflies usually quite quickly, in a matter of weeks or months. But the caterpillar of the Arctic Woolly Bear Moth is a slow developer. It stays as a caterpillar for 7-13 years!

Can you believe it?

The caterpillar is found in the icy north of Canada and Greenland. For much of the year it remains frozen but alive. It thaws out in the summer when it eats as many plants as it can before it freezes again!

WOW!

THE ARCTIC WOOLLY BEAR CATERPILLAR CAN SURVIVE TEMPERATURES AS LOW AS -60°C!

The furry caterpillar rests on a twig during summer.

MAYFLY

A mayfly starts life as an egg on the bed of the river. Then it hatches into a nymph, which lives in the water for up to two years before flying off as an adult mayfly. Many adult mayflies live for less than 24 hours.

This Drake Mackerel Mayfly is common in parts of Britain in the summer time.

Can you believe it?

There are 2,000 different species of mayfly. All seek out a mate with which to breed, and then die shortly afterwards. Some female adult mayflies live for less than 10 minutes!

CONTENDERS

The Hessian fly lives for just four days, whilst some parasitoid wasps have a life of only three days.

15

SOUTHERN GIANT DARNER

Dragonflies are rapid movers through the air. This large dragonfly, which lives around streams and fallen logs in Australia, is believed to be the fastest insect of all, reaching speeds of 56km/h.

FASTEST FLIER!

Can you believe it?

A dragonfly's eyes cover almost their entire head and have about 30,000 lenses, giving it all-round vision.

With its bright blue body, the Southern Giant Darner stands out against the background.

CONTENDERS

Some types of Hawk Moth (right) have been measured flying at speeds of between 40 and 53km/h.

ILLACME PLENIPES

Found in the United States, Illacme plenipes is the leggiest bug of all. It is a type of millipede that can grow as many as 750 short legs!

Can you believe it?

Despite all those legs, this millipede is less than 3cm long and has an almost see-through body. It has no eyes and lives underground around 10-15cm deep in soil.

WOW!

HAIRS ON THE BODY OF ILLACME PLENIPES PRODUCE SILK, WHICH HELPS THE CREATURE CLING TO ROCKS.

This Illacme plenipes has 618 legs. Imagine counting them all!

CHAN'S MEGASTICK

Forget your 4cm-long cockroach or a 5cm beetle, Chan's megastick is a whopper! Found only in some forests in Borneo, its body alone measures around 35cm. Add its long, thin legs, and the creature measures 55cm. That's one big bug!

LONGEST INSECT!

Can you believe it?

You'd think something so large would be well known, but Chan's megastick was only named in 2008. It was called Chan after amateur insect collector, Datuk Chan Chew Lun, who'd found a sample of the creature a few years earlier.

WOW!

THE EGGS OF A CHAN'S MEGASTICK ARE ODDLY SHAPED WITH LITTLE CURVED WINGS ON THEIR SIDES. THESE HELP AN EGG CATCH THE WIND AND FLY AWAY FROM WHERE THE MOTHER DROPS THEM.

Datuk Chan Chew Lun holds an example of the megastick insect named after him.

QUEEN ALEXANDRA'S BIRDWING

Male Queen Alexandra's birdwings have a huge wingspan of up to 20cm, but females are even bigger. They can measure up to 30cm from wingtip to wingtip. Hold up your ruler and imagine a butterfly as wide as that!

Can you believe it?

These giant butterflies are only found in a tiny area of forest in Papua New Guinea. The female butterfly (below) lays 4mm-long eggs on the tops of 40m-tall trees.

The butterfly's 8cm-long body is dwarfed by its giant wings.

On the other hand...

The Sinai Baton Blue butterfly (above left) measures just 10mm across. It's only found on Mount Sinai in Egypt.

HERCULES BEETLE

These big bugs grow up to 17cm long and are incredibly strong. The male beetles can lift up to 800 times their own bodyweight using their horn-like pincers. That's like you lifting a box containing six elephants!

Whoah! One male Hercules beetles lifts another into the air during a fight.

Can you believe it?

Hercules beetles are found in the rainforests of Central and South America. The males use their lifting power against each other when fighting for a mate. They battle, trying to flip each other over with their pincers.

A leafcutter ant carries a leaf back to a nest that may hold over five million ants.

CONTENDERS

Dung beetles (left) can move objects 1,000 times their weight but cannot lift as much weight up in the air as Hercules beetles. Leafcutter ants (above) carry parts of plants more than 50 times their own bodyweight to build their nests.

A dung beetle rolls a large ball of dung. Some beetles steal others' dung balls!

WORKER HONEY BEE

Despite only living for 42 days, no other insects have as many different jobs during their short lives as worker honey bees. They start off as cleaners in their hive, then undertakers, removing dead bees from the hive. They switch jobs to nurse infant bees before becoming couriers and collecting nectar from other bees that have flown out into fields.

MOST JOBS!

Can you believe it?

Worker bees also act as air conditioners, using their wings to fan the air in a hive to keep it moving. Once they're 12 days old they start making beeswax, which they use to repair the hive and build new parts.

Busy bees clean and repair the six-sided cells that make up the honeycombs inside their hive.

A bee collects pollen from a flower, storing it in pollen baskets on its back legs.

When they're about three weeks old, they become an apprentice field bee. They follow other, older bees on flights to flowers where they gather pollen and nectar to help feed the hive.

WOW!

BEES HAVE TO MAKE AROUND 2 MILLION VISITS TO FLOWERS TO MAKE ENOUGH HONEY TO FILL A 450G JAR.

COLLEMBOLA (SPRINGTAILS)

You might think it was the house fly or flea, but bug scientists reckon that Collembola (also known as springtails) are the most common bug of all. These live in the soil or amongst the leaves on a forest floor.

MOST COMMON!

Can you believe it?

A single square metre of soil has been found to hold as many as 200,000 springtails. This equals billions and billions of them around the world.

Springtails grow to between 1mm and 6mm long.

Springtails get their common name from a tail-like part called a furcula. They use it to help them spring away from danger.

On the other hand...

The rarest insect is Lord Howe's stick insect. It was thought to have died out until 2001 when just 24 were found on an island off the coast of Australia.

ANOPHELES MOSQUITO

The most deadly insect to humans doesn't have giant fangs or powerful venom. Anopheles mosquitoes are dangerous because they carry and transmit malaria. This disease infects over 200 million people and kills more than 660,000 every year.

MOST DANGEROUS TO HUMANS!

A blood-sucking female mosquito on human skin.

Can you believe it?

Only female mosquitoes suck blood from humans using their needle-like mouthparts to pierce the skin. Their rear body, called the abdomen, swells red with the blood it sucks up.

CONTENDERS

Tsetse flies, which live in Africa, spread a deadly disease known as sleeping sickness. This disease kills more than 200,000 people every year.

BRAZILIAN WANDERING SPIDER

MOST VENOMOUS!

Found in Central and South America, this spider is large with a leg span of 15cm, and it's lethal too! The venom in a single spider would be enough to kill more than 150 mice.

Can you believe it?

It is nicknamed the banana spider for its habit of stowing away in shipments of fruit. In 2008, a supermarket in Chatham, England had to close because one was found in a box of bananas!

The spider preys on lizards, mice and large insects. Its venom is over 10 times more powerful than that of a black widow spider (see page 27).

On the other hand...

Bagheera kiplingi is almost entirely vegetarian, the only spider that is. The only meat that the spider tends to eat is of other Bagheera kiplingi spiders. Yes, the spider is a cannibal!

CONTENDERS

The venom of the black widow spider is 15 times more powerful than a rattlesnake's venom. The female sometimes kills and eats the male spider after the two have mated.

Beware! A female black widow patrols her web.

DESERT LOCUST

Desert locusts fly together in large swarms. These hungry bugs can devastate crops as, every day, they can eat their entire bodyweight in food.

BIGGEST BUG SWARM!

Can you believe it?

A large swarm can involve more than a 1,000 million locusts and cover hundreds of square kilometres. Together, these can scoff thousands of kilograms of crops in a single day.

A swarm of desert locusts in Senegal, Africa. These pests may even eat their way through the straw houses in which some African farmers live.

Adult desert locusts vary in size from 1.2 to 7cm long. They have two pairs of wings that overlap and allow them to fly long distances. On the ground they can walk or jump using their extra-long pair of legs at the back.

A desert locust has wings and six legs. Using its rear legs, it can hop up to 50-70cm off the ground.

WOW!

PEOPLE IN SOME COUNTRIES IN ASIA AND AFRICA GET THEIR OWN BACK ON LOCUSTS FOR EATING THEIR CROPS BY DEEP-FRYING AND EATING THEM AS A CRUNCHY TREAT!

TEST YOURSELF!

Can you remember all the facts about the record-busting bugs in this book? Test yourself here by answering these questions!

1. Which insect is louder: a water boatman or an African cicada?

2. What type of ant can lift up pieces of plant more than 50 times its own bodyweight?

3. What sort of fruit is the Brazilian wandering spider sometimes found amongst?

4. Does a worker honey bee live for 24 hours, 12 days, 42 days or 14 years?

5. Which creature builds nests that can stand over 6m in height?

6. Would you find a Giant Southern Darner: in Africa, North America or Australia?

7. Which bug's eggs have little curved wings on their shells?

8. In which continent would you find Goliath bird eating spiders?

9. Which spider's venom is 15 times more powerful than a rattlesnake's?

10. Which butterfly has a wingspan of 30cm?

Answers
1. African cicada
2. Leafcutter ant
3. Bananas
4. 42 days
5. Termites
6. Australia
7. Chan's megastick
8. South America
9. Black widow spider
10. Queen Alexandra's birdwing

BUT WHAT DOES THAT MEAN?

abdomen The rear part of an insect's body usually containing its heart and parts which digest its food.

amateur Someone who does something as a hobby rather than as a paid job.

apprentice A trainee worker.

catapult To launch or fling something often with great power or speed.

couriers Those that carry either messages or objects from one place to another.

decibels A measure of the loudness of a sound.

hibernate To be inactive for a long time during a winter to save energy.

malaria A dangerous disease that is spread by mosquitoes.

membranes A thin skin or covering.

nectar A sugary, sweet liquid collected by some bugs and birds from flowers.

nymph A stage in the life of many insects before they become fully-grown adults.

parasitoid Types of insect whose babies live on or inside another creature and feed off it.

periodical Describes something that happens after a regular period of time, such as cicadas coming out of the ground after a number of years.

pincers A type of two-pointed claw found on some bugs, used for grabbing, gripping and pulling.

pollen Yellow powder inside flowers which contains the male cells used in making new flowers.

predators Creatures that hunt and eat other creatures.

species A type of living thing.

swarm A large number of bugs all moving together.

undertakers Those who prepare dead bodies.

venom A poisonous liquid.

wingspan The distance across stretched-out wings, measured from the tip of one wing to the other.

CHECK IT OUT & INDEX

Check out these amazing places to go and websites to visit!

The Bug House, World Museum, Liverpool, UK
Here you can see live ants, beetles, bees and other bugs as well as Avril the giant mechanical spider that lives on the museum's ceiling.

Insect Zoo at the Natural History Museum of Los Angeles County, USA
Check out all the living bugs from centipedes to giant spiders at this great live exhibit.

Australian Museum, Sydney, Australia
See cicadas, funnel-web spiders and many more bugs here.

http://www.uksafari.com/creepycrawlies.htm
Go on a bug safari in the UK with this handy guide with lots of pictures and facts.

http://www.enchantedlearning.com/themes /insects.shtml
Lots of facts and fun things to do about insects from rhymes to puzzles at this website.

http://www.amentsoc.org/bug-club/
A club for kids interested in all sorts of bugs. The website has lots of fun facts and activities for non-members, too.

Index